Lively Plant Science Projects

ANN BENBOW AND COLIN MABLY

ILLUSTRATIONS BY TOM LABAFF

Enslow Elementary

an imprint of

Enslow Publishers, Inc.
40 Industrial Road
Box 398
Berkeley Heights, NJ 07922
USA

http://www.enslow.com

Enslow Elementary, an imprint of Enslow Publishers, Inc.

Enslow Elementary® is a registered trademark of Enslow Publishers, Inc.

Library of Congress Cataloging-in-Publication Data

Benbow, Ann.
    Lively plant science projects / Ann Benbow and Colin Mably.
      p. cm. — (Real life science experiments)
    Includes bibliographical references and index.
    Summary: "Presents several easy-to-do science experiments using plants" Provided by publisher.
    ISBN-13: 978-0-7660-3146-3
    ISBN-10: 0-7660-3146-2
    1. Botany—projects—Juvenile literature. 2. BotanyISBN-10: 0-7660-3146-2
    Experiments—Juvenile literature. 3. Plants—Experiments—Juvenile literature. I. Mably, Colin. II. Title.
    QK52.6.B46 2009
    580.78—dc22
                                  2008001745

Printed in the United States of America
042010 Lake Book Manufacturing, Inc., Melrose Park, IL
10 9 8 7 6 5 4 3 2

To Our Readers: We have done our best to make sure all Internet Addresses in this book were active and appropriate when we went to press. However, the authors and the publisher have no control over and assume no liability for the material available on those Internet sites or on other Web sites they may link to. Any comments or suggestions can be sent by e-mail to comments@enslow.com or to the address on the back cover.

♻ Enslow Publishers, Inc., is committed to printing our books on recycled paper. The paper in every book contains 10% to 30% post-consumer waste (PCW). The cover board on the outside of each book contains 100% PCW. Our goal is to do our part to help young people and the environment too!

Illustration Credits: Tom LaBaff

Photo Credits: © Paige Falk/iStockphoto.com, p. 36; © Lowell Gordon/iStockphoto.com, p. 44; © Richard Carlton/Visuals Unlimited, p. 12; © Robert Churchill/iStockphoto.com, p. 24; Shutterstock, pp. 8, 16, 20, 28, 32; USDA Photo by Ken Hammond, p. 40.

Cover Photo: Shutterstock

Contents

Experiments with a 🎀 symbol feature **Ideas for Your Science Fair.**

Introduction

Plants are everywhere! They are one of the main groups of living things. Plants are special because they can make their own food. They are also a food source for other living things.

Plants that you might know include grasses, roses, oak trees, sunflowers, spruce trees, ferns, and mosses. People use many plant parts for food. We eat stems (asparagus), leaves (lettuce), fruits (apple), roots (carrot), flowers (broccoli tops), and seeds (peas).

You can use this book to investigate many things about plants. You'll be asking questions about plants and doing experiments with them. You'll make observations and find answers. By the end, you'll know a lot more about plants than you do now. You will also know more about science!

Science Fair Ideas

The investigations in this book will help you learn how to do experiments. After every investigation, you will find ideas for science fair projects. You may want to try one of these ideas, or you might think of a better project.

This book has a Learn More section. The books and Web sites in this section can help you with science fair projects.

Remember, science is all about asking questions. A science fair gives you the chance to investigate your own questions and record your results. It also lets you share your findings with your fellow scientists.

Safety First!

These are important rules to follow as you experiment.

1 Always have an adult nearby when doing experiments.

2 Follow instructions with care, especially safety warnings.

3 Never experiment with electrical outlets.

4 Use safety scissors and have an adult handle any sharp objects.

5 Use only alcohol thermometers, never mercury!

6 Stay in a safe place if making outdoor observations.

7 Treat living things with care. Some may sting or be poisonous!

8 Keep your work area clean and organized.

9 Clean up and put materials away when you are done.

10 Always wash your hands when you are finished.

Experiment 1
What Do Plants Do Without Water?

What do you think happens to a plant when it doesn't get watered? Write down your ideas and your reasons for them.

Now Let's Find Out!

1 On the first day of your experiment, label one Plant A and the other Plant B. Feel the soil in each plant to see if it is moist. Also, observe the leaves of both plants. Do they look fresh and healthy? Write or draw your observations about the plants.

Things You Will Need

2 potted plants, same size

water

measuring cup

pencil and paper

indoor sunny area

2 Add the same amount of water to each plant, just until the soil feels moist. Put the plants in a sunny spot (like a window) and leave them alone until the next day.

3   On the second day, feel the soil of Plant A to see if it is moist. If not, add a small amount of water. Do not add water to Plant B.

4   Add a small amount of water every day to Plant A. Add no water to Plant B. Record your observations of both plants each day. By the end of the week, what has happened to Plant B? Why do you think that happened?

5   What do you think you could do to make both plants the same as they were when you started?

What Do Plants Do Without Water?
An Explanation

Just like other living things, plants need water to stay alive. Water enters a plants through its roots. When you do not water a plant, its leaves begin to droop. This is because the water in the leaves evaporates into the air. This happens through tiny holes on the underside of the leaves.

FACT: Some plants, especially those that grow in the desert, need very little water to stay alive. Cacti have roots that spread out to reach water in the ground. They also have very thick stems to store water and tiny holes in their leaves that can keep closed when the sun is hottest.

Cacti

If you do not water the plant for a long time, it will dry up and die.

Ideas for Your Science Fair

- What happens when you water a plant too much?
- Will plants survive if they are watered with salt water?
- Do plants with thick leaves (like aloe) need less water than plants with thin leaves (like petunias)?

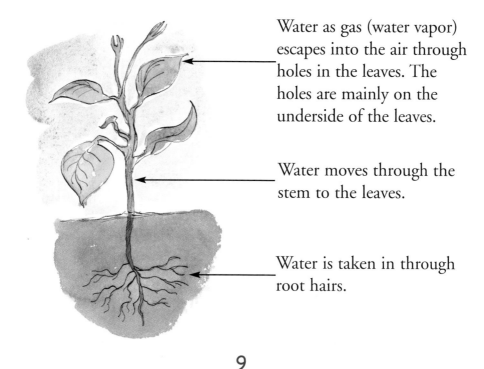

Water as gas (water vapor) escapes into the air through holes in the leaves. The holes are mainly on the underside of the leaves.

Water moves through the stem to the leaves.

Water is taken in through root hairs.

How Are Plants' Roots the Same and Different?

Do you think that all plants have the same types of roots? Write down your ideas and your reasons for them.

Now Let's Find Out!

1 Look at all your roots carefully with your magnifier. What similar parts do all the roots seem to have?

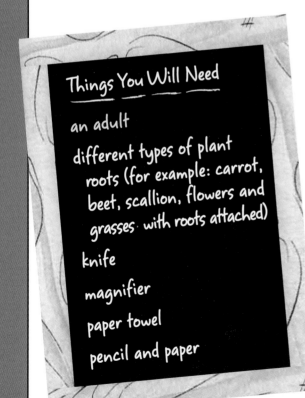

Things You Will Need

an adult

different types of plant roots (for example: carrot, beet, scallion, flowers and grasses. with roots attached)

knife

magnifier

paper towel

pencil and paper

2 **Ask an adult** to very carefully cut a carrot and beet open lengthwise. How are these two roots the same? How are they different?

3 Compare the carrot and beet to the roots of the flowers, grasses, and scallion.

How are they different? Write down your observations or draw pictures of the different roots.

4 Roots bring water and nutrients into plants. Which roots look like they could get water from deep in the soil? Which look like they would get water from higher up in the soil? Why do you think so?

How Are Plants' Roots the Same and Different?

An Explanation

There are many different kinds of roots, but all roots have an important job. They move water and nutrients from the soil into the plant through tiny "root hairs." Carrots and beets are taproots. Taproots are main roots with smaller roots growing off them. Taproots are usually found in plants like carrots, beets, and dandelions.

<u>FACT:</u> Some plants in rainforests have roots that never reach the ground. These roots collect moisture and nutrients from the air. Some types of orchids have these roots.

Orchid with roots

12

Plants such as grasses and onions have a different type of root. They are called fibrous roots. Fibrous roots spread out to gather water from a wider area.

 Ideas for Your Science Fair

- Which can be pulled out of the ground more easily: taproots or fibrous roots?

- How do plant roots keep soil from washing away?

- How are roots able to break through concrete?

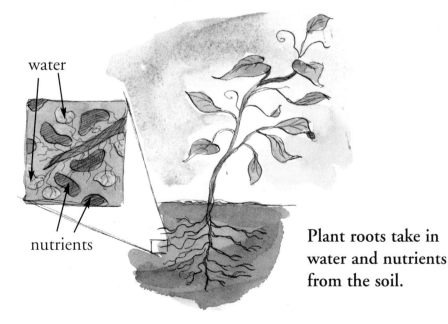

water

nutrients

Plant roots take in water and nutrients from the soil.

What Soil Is Best for Petunia Plants?

Do you think that a petunia plant will grow better in one soil than it will in another? Write down your ideas and your reasons for them.

Now Let's Find Out!

1 Open bags of potting soil and sand. Which has the smallest particles? Which has fertilizer added? Which feels more moist? Which type do you think would help the petunias to grow best? Why do you think that?

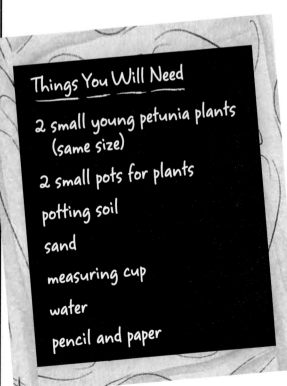

Things You Will Need

2 small young petunia plants (same size)

2 small pots for plants

potting soil

sand

measuring cup

water

pencil and paper

2 Fill one pot three-quarters full of potting soil. Fill the other pot three-quarters full of sand. Label each pot with its type of soil.

3   Shake the soil from the roots of each petunia. Plant one petunia in each pot. Add the same amount of water to each pot, enough to make the potting soil and sand moist.

4   Put the plants in a sunny place and observe them every day for at least two weeks. Be sure to water them the same amount every day. Write down and draw what you observe each day. Do the plant's leaves stay the same color? Do they get taller or shorter?

5   Continue your experiment for two more weeks. After that time, read over all your observations. Take a last look at your petunias. What conclusions can you draw about which soil is best for petunias? Why do you think that?

What Soil Is Best for Petunia Plants?

An Explanation

Petunias need soil that lets water pass through easily. Petunias also grow well with some nutrients added to the soil.

Potting soil is made of bark, peat moss, perlite, and nutrients. Water drains slowly through soil. Sand lets water through, but does not have nutrients added.

FACT: Most plants take nutrients from the soil to help them grow. Some plants, however, help put nutrients back into the soil. One example is peanuts. They help put nitrogen (one type of nutrient) into the soil.

Peanut plants

16

The petunias in the potting soil should have grown better than the petunias in the sand because potting soil lets water through easily and has nutrients.

 ## Ideas for Your Science Fair

- What soil mixture lets water pass through most quickly?

- Can petunias grow in water, or do they need to be planted in soil?

- Which soil holds water best: topsoil, potting soil, or garden soil?

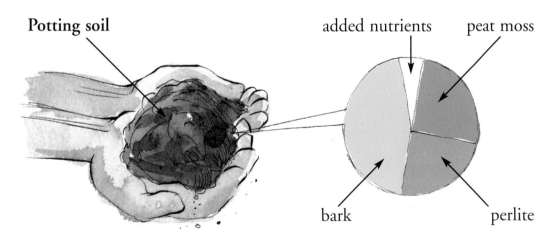

Experiment 4
How Does Water Travel Up a Plant?

How do you think water gets from a plant's roots to its leaves? Write down your ideas and your reasons for them.

Now Let's Find Out!

1 Before you begin the experiment, look carefully at your celery stalks. How do you think water can get from the base of the stalk to the leaves?

Things You Will Need

an adult

2 clear plastic cups

water

red food coloring

2 celery stalks

knife

pencil and paper

2 Fill two plastic cups three-quarters full of water. Add four drops of red food coloring to each cup. Take the leaves off only one of the stalks of celery. **Ask an adult** to cut the base of each stalk so that both stalks are the same length.

18

3 Put one stalk of celery into each and leave them overnight in a cool place. What do you think will happen and why?

4 The next day, observe your celery stalks. What happened to the celery in each of the cups? How do you think this happened? How was the stalk with the leaves different from the one without the leaves? Why do you think this was so?

5 **Ask an adult** to cut each piece of celery across about one inch (2.5 cm) from the base. What do you see inside each celery stalk? How can this help you to explain what happened to the celery?

How Does Water Travel Up a Plant?

An Explanation

Water travels up the stems of plants through tiny tubes. Water is able to do this because it is attracted to the sides of the tubes and to other water particles. At the same time, the plant is losing water through holes in the underside of its leaves. This loss of water through the leaves enables the

FACT: Plants put water back into the air through their leaves. A birch tree can put as much as 3,400 liters (900 gallons) of water back into the air every day through the tiny holes in its leaves.

Birch tree

water within the celery's tubes to move up the celery stalk. Without its leaves, the celery stalk cannot lose water and the colored water cannot move up.

Ideas for Your Science Fair

- Will colored water move up flower stems in the same way as it does with celery?

- Will hot water travel up stems more quickly or more slowly than cold water?

- If you take half the leaves off a stalk of celery, will colored water move up it more slowly than it will in a stalk with all of its leaves?

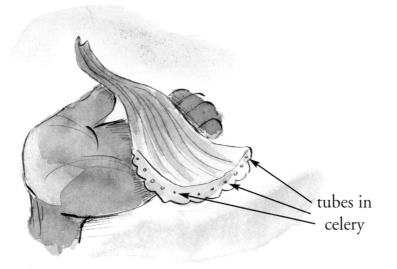

tubes in celery

Experiment 5
How Quickly Do Plants Grow?

Do you think that all plants grow at the same rate? Write down your ideas and your reasons for them.

Now Let's Find Out!

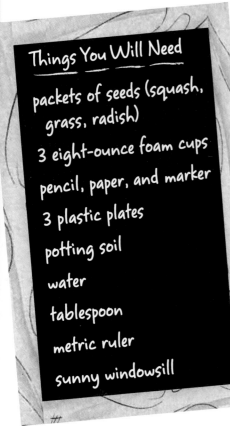

Things You Will Need

packets of seeds (squash, grass, radish)

3 eight-ounce foam cups

pencil, paper, and marker

3 plastic plates

potting soil

water

tablespoon

metric ruler

sunny windowsill

1 Using a pencil, punch four small holes into the bottoms of three 8-ounce foam cups. Fill the cups to the rim with potting soil. Label each cup with the name of the seed that it will contain.

2 Read each seed packet to find out how deeply to plant the seeds in the soil. Plant three seeds in each cup. Place the cups on top of a plastic plate to collect water coming out of the holes.

3 Measure two tablespoons of water for each cup and sprinkle the water over the seeds.

4 On your piece of paper, write down the date, the types of seeds, and the amount of water you put on each. Put the cups and plates into a sunny area, such as a windowsill.

5 Each day, feel the soil. If it feels dry, add another two tablespoons of water to each cup. On your paper, record the date and the amount of water you added.

6 When the plants begin to sprout, measure in centimeters how high they are each day for two weeks. Record the date and heights on your paper for each plant.

How Quickly Do Plants Grow?

An Explanation

Not all plants grow at the same rate. One reason is that there are chemicals inside the plants. These chemicals control how rapidly the plants grow when they have just the right amount of light, heat, water, and nutrients. Another reason is that plants do not grow as quickly if they do not have enough water or sunlight.

Plants also need certain types of soil to grow best. Grass

FACT: Some bamboo plants can grow as much as one meter (about one yard) a day. One type of bamboo can grow more than 200 meters (about 70 feet) tall.

Bamboo plants

usually grows very quickly, but even different types of grasses grow at different rates. Radishes will usually grow a little more slowly than grasses. Of the three plants you tested, the squash probably grew most slowly.

 ## Ideas for Your Science Fair

- In what ways does the amount of light affect how quickly radish plants grow?

- Does the amount of water affect how rapidly grass plants grow?

- How does the type of soil affect how quickly squash plants grow?

How Are Plants' Leaves the Same and Different?

In what ways are leaves the same and different? Write down your ideas and your reasons for them.

Now Let's Find Out!

1 Look at all your leaves with your magnifier. Be sure to look on both sides of each leaf. What are similar parts that all the leaves seem to have? Are they all the same shape? Do they all have stems? How are the leaves different?

2 Draw each of the leaves and label their parts, using the leaf diagram on the next page as a guide.

3 What leaf parts do you think help move water through the leaf? Why do you think so?

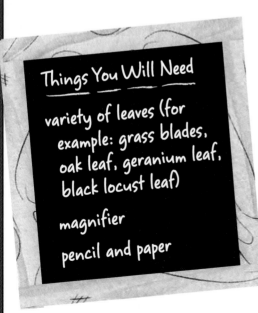

Things You Will Need

variety of leaves (for example: grass blades, oak leaf, geranium leaf, black locust leaf)

magnifier

pencil and paper

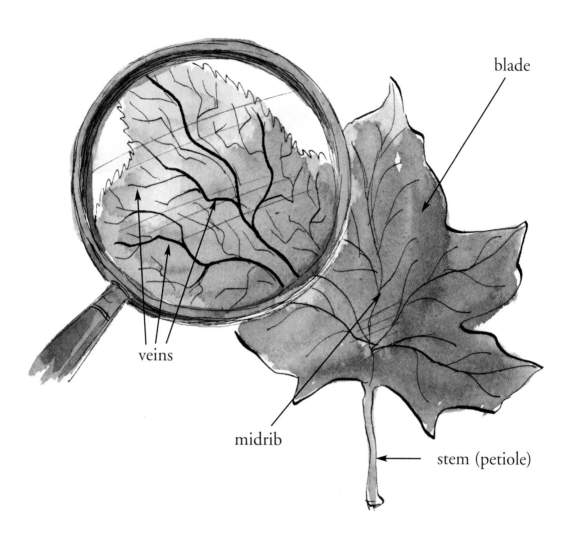

blade

veins

midrib

stem (petiole)

4 What leaf parts let water escape from the leaf? What parts do you think have the green chemical that helps plants make their own food?

How Are Plants' Leaves the Same and Different?

An Explanation

The leaves of just about all plants contain a green substance called chlorophyll. It helps plants make their own food. Chlorophyll is inside the cells of a leaf.

Other similar things are the veins (lines in the leaves), the tiny bumps on the underside (stomata), and the stem (petiole). The veins help the water move through the leaf.

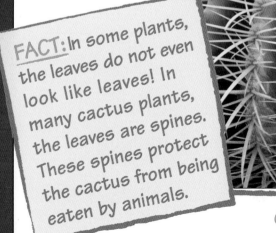

FACT: In some plants, the leaves do not even look like leaves! In many cactus plants, the leaves are spines. These spines protect the cactus from being eaten by animals.

Cactus plant with spines

The stomata are tiny holes that let water out of the leaf.

Leaves can be many shapes, sizes, and thicknesses, but most leaves are darker on the top than on the underside.

 ## Ideas for Your Science Fair

- Will a leaf sprout to make roots if you put it in water?

- If you covered the stomata of a leaf with petroleum jelly, what would happen to the leaf?

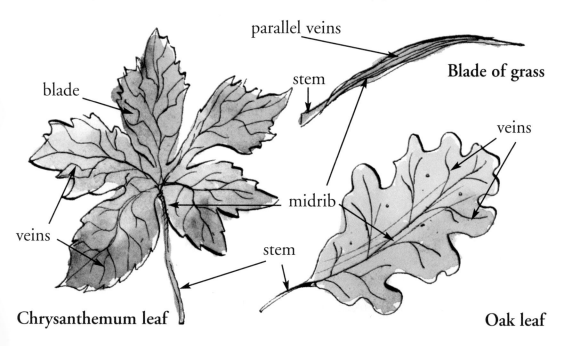

parallel veins

stem

Blade of grass

blade

veins

veins

midrib

stem

Chrysanthemum leaf

Oak leaf

Experiment 7
How Can Flower Petal Colors Be Changed?

How can you make colors from flower petals change? Write down your ideas and your reasons for them.

Now Let's Find Out!

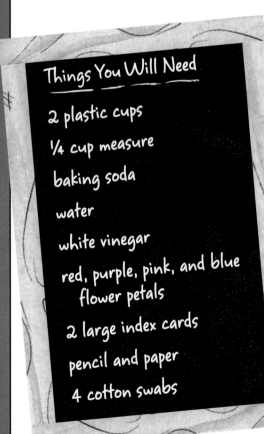

Things You Will Need

- 2 plastic cups
- ¼ cup measure
- baking soda
- water
- white vinegar
- red, purple, pink, and blue flower petals
- 2 large index cards
- pencil and paper
- 4 cotton swabs

1 In one plastic cup, dissolve a tablespoon of baking soda in ¼ cup of water. Put ¼ cup of white vinegar in the other cup.

2 Look at your collection of flower petals. (You may want to ask a local florist for some samples to help you with your experiment.) How do you think you could make the petals change color? Write down your ideas.

baking soda

vinegar

3 Use a pencil to divide an index card into four sections. Print the color of each of the four kinds of petals on the bottom of each section.

4 Bunch one color of flower petals between your fingers (like you would hold a crayon). Rub the petals hard on the section of the index card for that color.

5 Dip one end of a cotton swab into the vinegar and "paint" over one third of each of the color sections. What happens to the color? In the same way, paint over another third with a cotton swab dipped into the baking soda water. What happens here? Record your observations.

How Can Flower Petal Colors Be Changed?

An Explanation

The colors from some flower petals are able to be changed when you add certain chemicals to them. These chemicals are acids (like vinegar) and bases (like baking soda).

Colors that change with acids and bases are called "indicators." Usually blue and purple colors from petals

FACT: Early on, humans discovered they could use colorful plant parts to dye cloth for clothing. Some people still use natural dyes when they color holiday eggs or dye cloth. Onion skins, for example, can give a rich golden color.

Yarn colored with natural dyes

turn greenish with baking soda. With vinegar, they usually turn pinkish. Red or pink petal colors usually turn blue with bases and back to red or pink with acids.

Ideas for Your Science Fair

- Will the orange color from carrots change with vinegar and with baking soda?

- Does lemon juice act like vinegar or like baking soda with flower color indicators?

- What colored fruit juices change color with vinegar and with baking soda?

Vinegar (acid) ⟷ **Baking Soda** (base)

Experiment 8
Do Plants Move Toward Light?

What happens when plants are put in the dark and in the light? Write down your ideas and your reasons for them.

Now Let's Find Out!

1 Look carefully at your potted bean plants. In what direction are the stems growing? Write down your observations.

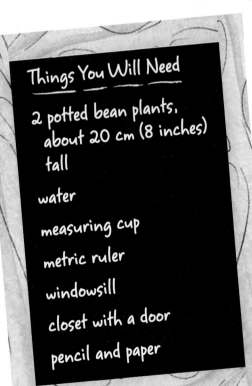

Things You Will Need

2 potted bean plants, about 20 cm (8 inches) tall

water

measuring cup

metric ruler

windowsill

closet with a door

pencil and paper

2 Make sure that both plants start out with the same amount of water (the soil should be moist). Put one plant on the windowsill and place the other in the closet. Leave the closet door open about 3 cm (a little more than 1 inch). What do you think will happen to the plants? Write down your prediction.

3 Every day for one week, observe both plants. Write down your observations about the direction the stems are growing and the color of the leaves. Make sure that both plants get watered when their soil feels dry.

4 After one week, what has happened to the stems and leaves of both plants? How did this fit with your prediction?

Do Plants Move Toward Light?

An Explanation

Almost all plants must have light to survive. They have ways of making sure they get all the light they need. Plants have chemicals in them that cause them to grow toward the light. As you probably saw with your experiment, the stems and leaves of the bean plant in the closet ended up facing the

FACT: Some plants respond so much to light that you can observe them in different positions during the day. The flowering stem of a yucca plant leans in different directions depending on where the sun is in the sky.

Yucca plant

little bit of light that came in through the door. It was trying to get the most amount of light it could by facing the light source. The windowsill plant had more available light, and did not need to turn as much.

 ## Ideas for Your Science Fair

- Are some plants more light-sensitive than others?
- What happens to a plant when it is kept in the dark all the time?
- Why do some flowers open at different times of the day?

Sunflowers turn toward the sun to get the most light.

How Well Do Plants Grow in Just Water?

Do you think that it is possible to grow plants in just water? Write down your ideas and your reasons for them.

Now Let's Find Out!

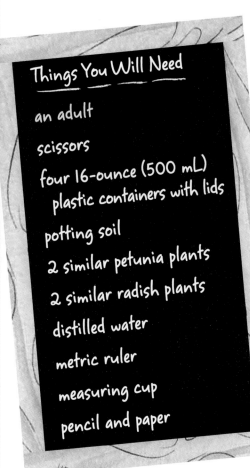

Things You Will Need

an adult

scissors

four 16-ounce (500 mL) plastic containers with lids

potting soil

2 similar petunia plants

2 similar radish plants

distilled water

metric ruler

measuring cup

pencil and paper

1 **Ask an adult** to carefully cut a 3-cm hole in two of the plastic lids and a 2-cm hole in the bottoms of two of the containers.

2 Fill the two containers with holes with potting soil. Plant a petunia in one container and a radish plant in the other. Put these containers on top of the plastic lids with no holes. Use the measuring cup to put in equal amounts of water.

38

cups with holes
in bottom

lids with
no holes

lids with
3-cm holes

cups with
water

3   Next fill the containers without holes with distilled water. Place the lids with the 3-cm holes on top. Wash the soil off the roots of a radish plant and a petunia plant. Slide the roots through the lid hole so that the roots are in the water while the stem and leaves sit above the lid.

4   Put all four cups in a sunny spot. Observe the plants for two weeks, and record your observations. Remember to water the "potting soil plants" when the soil feels dry.

5   Do both types of plants grow just as well in soil and in water? Explain your observations.

How Well Do Plants Grow in Just Water?

An Explanation

Plants need different kinds of nutrients to grow, as well as water and light. Three main nutrients that plants need to grow are chemicals called nitrogen, potassium, and phosphorus. If you try to grow plants in just water, without these nutrients, they do not have everything they need to grow.

FACT: Many different kinds of plants can grow in hydroponic liquids, including strawberries. It only takes about a half cup of water every day to grow a hydroponic strawberry plant. It takes much more water a day to grow a strawberry plant in the ground!

Hydroponic strawberries

There is a way of growing plants in water. It is called hydroponics. In hydroponics, plants are placed in a liquid that contains the right nutrients for them to grow and be healthy.

 ## Ideas for Your Science Fair

- Will plants grow better in sugar water than plain water?

- How well will plants grow in a mixture of half soil and half water?

- Which is better for plants: distilled water or tap water?

nutrients in liquid

Lettuce hydroponics kit

Experiment 10
How Are Plants Suited to Where They Live?

Why do different kinds of plants grow in different areas outside? Write down your ideas and your reasons for them.

Now Let's Find Out!

1 Go outside with your pad of paper and pencil. Draw a line down the center of the page. On the left side, draw plants you see growing in a sunny area. On the right side of the page, draw plants growing in a shady area.

2 What do plants that grow in shade seem to have in common? Look at the colors, sizes, and shapes of their leaves. Are their flowers large or small? Brightly colored or not? Are they completely in the shade, or do they get some sun, too?

Things You Will Need

yard, garden, park, or playground

pad of paper and pencil

3 What do plants that grow in the sun seem to have in common? Look at the colors, sizes, and shapes of their leaves. How do the sizes and colors of their flowers compare to the shade-loving plants?

4 Why do you think that shade-loving plants have the kinds of leaves they do? Why do sun-loving plants have the kinds of leaves they do?

How Are Plants Suited to Where They Live?

An Explanation

Some plants are suited to shady areas, while others do better growing in the sun. Still other plants survive in a mixture of sun and shade.

Shade-loving plants usually have wide, flat leaves. This is to catch as much sunlight as possible. Shade-loving plants also have smaller flowers than sun-loving plants.

FACT: Some plants bloom only at night. The moonflower has big white fragrant blossoms that open up when it gets dark.

Night-blooming moonflower

Sun-loving plants usually have small leaves that point toward the sun. The small leaves get more sun so they do not need to be bigger to catch the light.

 Ideas for Your Science Fair

- What happens to sun-loving plants when they are planted in shade?

- What happens to shade-loving plants when they are planted in full sun?

- What types of plants like what types of soil?

elephant ears

salvia

yucca

hostas

ivy

purslane

Shade

Sunshine

Words to Know

cell—The smallest unit of a living thing.

chemical—Materials made of tiny particles found in all parts of nature.

chlorophyll—A green pigment in plants that they use to make food.

evaporate—To change from a liquid into a gas.

fertilizer—Nutrients added to soil or water to help plants grow.

fibrous roots—Fine, very hairy root branches that spread out.

hydroponics—Growing plants in water and nutrients without soil.

nutrients—Chemicals that plants need to grow.

peat moss—Moss that is used as a natural plant food.

perlite—Material that holds water when added to soil.

root hairs—Structures on roots that take in water and nutrients.

roots—Plant parts that take in water and nutrients.

soil—A mixture of sand, clay, rocks, living and once living things, water, and air.

taproot—The main plant root with small roots growing off it.

water vapor—Water that is in its gas form.

Learn More

Books

Bochinski, Julianne Blair. *The Complete Workbook for Science Fair Projects*. Hoboken, NJ: Wiley, 2005.

Spilsbury, Louise and Richard. *Plant Classification*. Portsmouth, NH: Heineman/Raintree, 2003.

Spilsbury, Louise and Richard. *Plant Habitats*. Portsmouth, NH: Heineman/Raintree, 2002.

Spohn, Rebecca. *Ready, Set, Grow!: A Kid's Guide to Gardening*. Tucson, AZ: Good Year Books, 2007.

Internet Addresses

How Stuff Works. *Plant Activities For Kids*.
http://home.howstuffworks.com/plant-activities-for-kids.htm

My First Garden.
http://www.urbanext.uiuc.edu/firstgarden/index.html

Gardens Kids' Page.
http://www.usbg.gov/forkids.cfm

Index